LET ME ASK YOU THIS...

*How to Get the Answers You
Need to Achieve Financial
Freedom and Build a Legacy*

NANCY WALLACE-LAABS

Let Me Ask You This… -- 1st ed.

ISBN: 978-1-946694-40-9

Dedication

*I am blessed with a loving family who supports me
in every step of discovering who I am as a woman, wife,
mother, friend, cheerleader, and role model.*

*Thank you, Brian, Kelcie, and Zac
for always listening to my never-ending talk of real estate.*

*To all my friends who I am sure annoyed
with all my questions – I love you all!*

Table of Contents

INTRODUCTION

"Mom, Why Do You Ask So Many Questions?"

My entire life, I have annoyed people because I am always asking questions. I'm old school, and to me, *there are NO stupid questions*. After all, how are you supposed to find answers if you do not question, research, and maybe ask again? When I get a response, it might lead me to ask 20 more questions. Am I annoying? Nosy? OR could it be I am just downright curious?

If you are a person that asks a lot of questions – why do you ask questions? Do you want to learn more? Maybe part of you wants to be in control. I got to where I am today by asking questions. I was formerly the Director of Recruitment for the second-largest blood bank in the U.S. and then created a "job" for myself.

Today, I am writing everything I learned along the way, so hopefully, my question asking will help propel you or someone you know to want more from life and be more!

I always say, "The Fortune is in the questions you ask!" Sometimes we ask the same questions because we need to work on our listening skills, or we didn't understand what the person was trying to tell us. You must know *how* to ask the right questions to carve your path, establish metrics, and gain clarity and focus.

You Can Do Anything!

Why do we do anything? What propels us to take on projects that seem impossible, fill us with self-doubt, and cause others to call us crazy? *Can I do this? Should I do this? Will anyone care if I do this?* The most important lesson I've learned as a real estate investor is: **You can do anything!** You can have as much as you want and still have time for yourself, your family, and anything else you desire in life.

In this book, I share stories from the journey my husband, Brian, and I have been on as real estate investors —the successes, missteps, and mistakes. At times, it was rocky, scary, and just downright fun! The last few years have taught us to be steadfast on what we want our life to look like, and we have followed not only our hearts but our will to overcome many obstacles that life threw in our way. We hope you enjoy our story, and it gives you the knowledge, grit, and determination to make your life exactly what you want and deserve!

Over the years, Brian and I have flipped, wholesaled, and created notes through owner financing, but the bread and butter of our business are single-family rentals. I wrote this book while creating our *Profitable Landlord System* and have included tips and real-life case studies from our deals and experiences on the path to becoming Profitable Landlords in each chapter.

So, what makes me an expert on this subject? The only thing I have to offer you is the story of my experience. I went from being stuck in a 9-5 job that I didn't enjoy (with a boss who I didn't always agree with) to calling my own shots!

In 2005, our family relocated from Phoenix, AZ, to Dallas, TX. We were at an age where we were planning for future college expenses for five children and ensuring we would have enough money to retire.

We were fortunate enough to take advantage of the real estate boom in Phoenix, sold our home, and took a leap of faith and moved to Frisco, Texas. This real estate transaction was so successful that we decided to incorporate a wealth-building strategy using real estate into our retirement plan.

Brian and I held successful positions where team building, organizational, and time management skills became the threshold of our successful careers. These skills made the transition to full-time real estate investing seamless.

Since moving to Texas, we have acquired several single-family rental homes. We have also invested in many fix-and-flips (doing the rehab work ourselves or overseeing the work) and owner-financed a couple of projects. Ultimately, we decided the best strategy to build long-term wealth and leave a legacy for our family was owning single-family rentals.

We continue to grow our real estate business by incorporating wholesaling, flipping, and buying single-family homes in appreciating areas.

CHAPTER 1:
ACQUIRING PROFITABLE SELLERS

How Can You Acquire Wealth Through Real Estate Investing?

To acquire wealth and build a legacy for your family through real estate investing, you must purchase properties at below-market values. **A Profitable Seller** is a motivated, distressed party who needs to sell their home and cannot do it using traditional real estate methods (listing on the open market).

Acquiring Profitable Sellers

We found the first few properties we purchased on the Multiple Listing Service (MLS). At the time, the market was inundated, but fortunately, we were investing in the Dallas/Fort Worth area when it was considered a buyer's market. We learned over the years (and you will too as you develop and grow your real estate investments) to pay attention to the market and know when to buy, sell, or hold. We looked only for single-family 3BR/2BA houses after learning those types of properties rent in any market.

Without realizing it at the time, we were defining our ten risk indicators. Because it was a buyer's market, the "Days on Market" for our first few properties was over 90 days, and two had been vacant for six months. These properties also were in appreciating areas of the Dallas/ Fort Worth area, and we were focusing on Plano, Wylie, and McKinney, Texas, which were each 30 minutes one way from where we lived.

Since we buy from distressed sellers (motivated but experiencing a life change such as downsizing, relocating, divorce, and even death), every property we purchased needed repairs. If the roof had to be replaced or repaired, we would require the seller to file a claim with their insurance company to cover that cost. All of our rental properties had foundation and plumbing repairs.

We got at least three bids for repairs on each property while learning the typical costs for different types of repair. It took a bit more of our time, but in the end, we were confident about our pricing and learned which contractors were more upfront than others!

Profitable Risk Indicators

When purchasing properties, we evaluate specific criteria and assess the risk using a rating scale of 1-5, with 1 being the lowest (or least risk) and 5 the highest risk (greatest risk). The first three properties we purchased all fell within the acceptable range of our profitable risk indicators.

Appreciating Areas

We knew that buying properties in appreciating areas could build equity and increase wealth. We hit it out of the ballpark on this one. Today, we would rate this risk a "1" for these properties; it doesn't get any better!

Number of Bedrooms

All of the properties we purchased were 3BR/2BA homes. We knew that houses with at least three bedrooms would appeal to the widest range of potential tenants for this area, so this was a low risk.

Repair Costs

Address any condition that could affect the health and safety of a tenant. When analyzing the properties, we received estimates for the costs of the repairs needed. Then, we compared that amount to the price of the house. Since the repair costs were less than 10% of the purchase price of the property, we considered this a low risk.

Age

We determined that houses built between 1978 and 1988 meet our requirements because they often need a lot of repairs, which is a benefit to us when negotiating with sellers. Houses built before 1978 or after 2000 are riskier to us. For our first few houses, we stayed within our desired risk factor rating of "1."

Location

At first, we only wanted to purchase properties in areas located within 30 minutes, one way, of where we lived. We were literally investing in our backyard, which made self-management easier at the time. Also, being so close allowed us to keep eyes on the property and do walk-throughs, making them low risk.

Distressed Seller

Buying from a distressed seller often allows you to purchase the house at a discounted price. Each of our first three houses had distressed sellers for varying reasons: one family had to relocate for a job, the second house was a short sale, and the owners of the third house had passed away, and their children were selling it.

Days on Market

Each property had been on the market for more than 90 days, which is high and represents a "buyer's market." When there are more houses on the market than buyers, prices are lower, and you can purchase at a discount.

The description for one house that had been on the market for almost a year read: "House will smell better when the furniture and carpet are removed."

Profits

Fast forward ten years, the appreciation value for two of our first three properties doubled. We purchased each for $115,000, and the value of each property was over $200,000 last year. So, our net worth increased by $200,000 with just two rental properties – not to mention the cash flow during those ten years AND all of the tax advantages owning real estate gives you.

Short Sales

Our most distressed property to date was a short sale from Wells Fargo. The property was listed on the MLS, but no one was buying in that particular area. It was the smallest house in a well-known subdivision – a 1700 sq. ft. 3BR/2BA home in a great school district. There were few rentals in that area. We knew that a family who didn't want to buy a house would find this home desirable, especially with all the amenities the property offered, the schools, the community pool, and access to the golf course.

We learned some valuable lessons in this deal:

1. Short sales take a long time – even if the seller and buyer agree on all terms

2. Banks will ask you repeatedly for the same information, so you need to be organized and work with lenders that deal with short sales. Be prepared to re-submit your proof of income, tax returns, etc.

3. This was the first rental property we purchased and then leased back to the seller. We made the mistake of not withholding part of the seller's proceeds at closing. When the seller moved out, he left trash everywhere, and we had to pay someone to clean up and haul the trash away. Their dogs also tore up

the fence and yard. ALWAYS hold $5,000-$10,000 from the seller's proceeds until they completely vacate the property AND you have verified it was left it in the condition specified in the sales contract.

After completing repairs to the foundation, plumbing, flooring, and painting, we rented the property within two days. Here is a breakdown of the costs:

Purchase Price	$140,000
Rehab	$10,000
Down Payment	$20,000
Loan*	**$110,000**
Monthly Payments	$884
Taxes	$291
Insurance	$83
HOA	$58
Total Payment	**$1316**

*Since the house appraised for $185,000, the lender let us put down $20,000, which was not quite 15%. Your relationship with your lenders is key to being a profitable landlord.

We rented this property for $1500/month the first year, and our cash flow was just under $200/month. As a profitable landlord, we increase our net worth not on the monthly cash flow but the following two things:

1. Appreciation

2. Mortgage buy down – from rent payments

Five years after we purchased the property, the value soared to $300,000, adding $160,000 of equity and net worth. In five years, our rental properties increased our net worth to over a million dollars.

We rinsed and repeated to continue building our net worth. Using the steps outlined in the Profitable Landlord System to find, fund, and manage our properties, we were able to create and build on our financial freedom!

Once we saw that the risk factors we focused on in our initial search for investment properties were paying off, we continued to use them to build our rental portfolio.

Finding the Deals

Listed below are a few examples of how I found some of my deals. I am genuinely transparent when it comes to marketing. There are plenty of deals for everyone, regardless of your market, regardless of how many other real estate investors are in your area, you can do this. Be consistent in your marketing – you won't get deals without it. Marketing is achieved in several ways, such as:

Referrals

This is by far my best way to get deals. It is cost-effective and verifies that you are building a reputation as someone who is trustworthy and gets the job done. So, your first order of business is to tell everyone you know what you are doing and what type of properties you are looking for.

Direct Mail

My second-best lead source is direct marketing, such as letters, postcards, and notecards. The message has changed over the years, but I have found it is best to keep it simple! Timing also plays a part in direct mail campaigns. If you are mailing to the same list other investors are using, realize that the recipient has been inundated with mailers and flyers. Sometimes, it is just the right time for them to sell, and your marketing message landed in their hands that day. One of the deals that I frequently speak about resulted from a postcard that a non-owner occupied received. The property had been vacant for five years, and I was not the only investor that had mailed, called, or contacted him. The day he got my card was the day he wanted to sell. I got the property under contract sight unseen for $10,000!

DRIVING FOR DOLLARS

Whenever I drive anywhere, I take 5-10 minutes to go through a neighborhood to look for distressed homes. I have an ongoing list of properties that might be unique to me (unless other investors are driving around the same areas as well). I purchased one property after driving through neighborhood. The house was appeared very distressed and had a realtor sign in the yard. I contacted the realtor to see the property and found out it was not yet listed on the MLS. I was the first investor to look at it. The seller was motivated because he had tried to sell the property the prior year, and it sat on the market for over 200 days! We made an offer on the spot, got it under contract, and now it is one of our best performing rental properties.

COLD CALLING

This type of marketing is not for the faint of heart or brand-new investors. First, you need to know how to "scrub" a call list so that you don't find yourself getting fined for calling folks on the DO NOT CALL LIST. I applied everything that I had designed, defined, and implemented, from setting up call centers while working at the blood bank to real estate investing. I hired staff to make the calls, and I set up KPIs, call times, and goal setting. I provided calling scripts, job aides, and scrubbed lists, and we were off and running. I have been yelled at and asked to remove names from the list, which we always do when asked, but those numbers are small for the lead generation and deal flow cold calling provided.

At the end of the chapter, there is a link so you can download my messaging and start using it today!

Marketing Strategies for Every Lead

When we develop a marketing strategy, we don't focus only on buying rental properties. Real estate investors should monetize each lead, not only leads that may make a good rental. We look at each property and evaluate it based on our current situation (cash flow, number of deals in the pipeline, etc.) to determine the best strategy for a lead.

In addition to age, location, and floor plan layout (yes, that is a thing!), we monetize every lead by looking at different exit strategies for each property. In the Profitable Landlord System, we focus on buying and holding, but you will learn, as we did, not every property fits our criteria. We still have an opportunity to profit on our lead through other strategies, such as wholesaling or owner financing.

Many variables go into our exit strategy decision. Our long-term wealth and financial freedom are primarily focused on single-family rentals, but we don't turn down an opportunity on any lead that comes our way. First and foremost, we love the idea of helping a distressed seller. Second, we recognize there is a motivated seller who needs to get out from under a property that is weighing them down financially and often emotionally. Third, we fix up these distressed properties ourselves, or sell them to someone who will fix it up. It is a win-win for the community, as a house that needed some attention and is an eyesore is now getting a much-needed facelift.

Bottom line: a seasoned real estate investor will know the steps to take to not only analyze the deal, but can monetize the lead, which offsets marketing costs, puts some money in your pocket, helps out a distressed seller, and improves a community one house at a time!

CASE STUDY
Growing a List of Profitable Sellers

One of the best ways to grow a database of profitable sellers is to *always* treat your sellers with respect and put their needs first. Sure, it is exciting to think you might get a property under contract at a considerable discount; after all, that is how we make our money. In one deal, I gave the seller a bit more, and in return, I got back more than double the amount.

Ms. Rhonda received a card in the mail and called me a year later about her property. I visited the house and saw that it needed very few repairs, mostly cosmetic. After an inspection to confirm the property was indeed in good shape, I made a fair offer that she accepted after some negotiating, and we scheduled the closing.

On the way to sign the papers, Ms. Rhonda called to tell me that her husband (who owned the property) was upset because he thought they were getting $4,000 more for the house than what the papers showed.

I could have held them to the contractual price that they had agreed to initially. However, I didn't want to have distressed sellers upset with me and feel that I had taken advantage of them. The cost of a negative review far outweighs a $4,000 price difference. So, at the last minute, we gave the sellers an additional $4,000, which cut into my "profit" on the buy. Since I planned to keep the house as a rental, I knew I had time to make up the $4,000.

Ms. Rhonda and her husband were so happy with the transaction that they referred one of their friends to me, and I made a $20,000 profit on the sale of that house.

So, that day I lost $4,000 — or you could say I "invested" it in future earnings, which I recouped within six months. Also, I have great reviews from two satisfied and profitable sellers!

Key Takeaways

❖ Time – I invested the time to do the marketing and had a profitable seller after 12 months.

❖ Value – I built a solid relationship with the seller and provided value to them for the sale of their property. In turn, I received a referral that provided significant value to me.

❖ Relationships – I continue to follow-up with these two sellers to maintain my relationship with them.

Finding Profitable Sellers with the Profitable Landlord System

The *Profitable Landlord System* will show you how to find and market to homeowners who want to sell their property. It takes time, consistency, follow-up, and perseverance. A profitable landlord must identify the right property, at the right price, and the right location to meet their needs.

To find profitable sellers, we incorporate different ongoing marketing campaigns, such as driving for dollars, referrals, and direct mail. We want to help you start your deal flow, so visit the link below to download a list of no-cost or low-cost marketing ideas and messaging you can implement today!

https://mailchi.mp/kbnhomes.com/qtnb5c13oe

Bonus Strategy

We rarely escrow the taxes and insurance and pay the property taxes for all of our properties at the end of the year.

Doing this allows me to keep my funds fluid. I might be able to deploy those funds that would otherwise be tied up at a mortgage company to passively invest as a private money lender. I am always in favor of making my money work for me.

During the 12-month period, I have the opportunity to utilize these funds and realize earnings of 8-10 percent.

However, a word of caution if you choose to do the same—ALWAYS set aside enough to cover the cost of the property taxes each month. Make sure you can manage this part of your business. If you don't think you can handle this each month, then escrow your property tax payments to avoid coming up short at the end of the year!

CHAPTER 2:
FINDING PROFITABLE TENANTS

DISCLAIMER: It is assumed that the reader is familiar with and will adhere to all Fair Housing Laws and will not discriminate based on Race, Color, National Origin, Sex, Familial Status, Disability.

After over a decade as a property manager, managing more than 1,000 doors, I have gained insight into what makes a tenant profitable for a landlord. Make no mistake – if you purchase the best property at the best price in the best location, you will not be a profitable landlord if you pick the wrong tenant.

When I first started as a real estate investor, I learned from my mentor that having long-term tenants can reduce my churn costs and allow me to maintain cash flow for years instead of only 12 months. The average tenant stays in our properties for four years, and some for over a decade.

Some people prefer to rent. When evaluating tenants for my properties, I purposefully look for someone who plans to live there for a while before buying a house OR has a strong rental history. Tenants that fit this category help reduce turnover and make-ready costs and offer consistent monthly cash flow, year after year, while paying down my mortgage.

One of our passions is to provide affordable housing. Everyone should have a roof over their head, a place to lay their head at night, and a safe environment in which they can raise their families.

CASE STUDY – LONG-TERM TENANTS

Our first tenant, Marcus, and his family rented a house from us for 11 years. We saw his two daughters grow up, move out, and start their own lives during that time.

The relationship was always professional, but if someone rents from you for multiple years, you will naturally learn about their family.

Marcos paid the rent through the entire lease period. During that time, the family faced one major financial interruption, but we were able to work out an agreement that was beneficial to both parties. Marcos and his family continued to have a place to live, and we as landlords had a tenant that made good on all of their rental agreements over the years.

Because of Marcos' continued payments, we paid off this property and were able to refinance, pull out the equity, and buy more rental properties.

KEY Mistakes Landlords Make When Finding and Retaining Profitable Tenants

1. Failure to apply appropriate screening criteria to all potential tenants

2. Inconsistent screening methods

3. Accepting the first applicant to fill a vacancy

4. Setting the rent too high for a given area

5. Getting too friendly with a tenant

PROPERLY SCREEN ALL APPLICANTS

Property managers follow a specific protocol and process to find and screen applicants for properties. When you purchase your first rental property, you will not have the same liability as a property management company or a real estate broker. But consistency in your screening process is a must whether you have one property or hundreds!

LANDLORDS beware! If you screen applicants differently each time, you could be opening yourself up to a discrimination suit. ALWAYS run background checks, collect information, and disclose all information in the same manner for each applicant.

The number one problem landlords bring to me is they have allowed a tenant to move in before doing a thorough background check AND without receiving certified funds. I have received many calls from distressed landlords who accepted a check and gave the applicant keys, allowing them to move into the house. Days later, they found out the check was no good and now must "evict" the person living in their property. Even worse, many fail to collect a signed lease agreement, which makes getting the person out of their property even more difficult. It happens too many times for first-time landlords.

The second most common problem I see landlords make is allowing a tenant early access to the property prior to the lease start date. It's not uncommon for tenants to request to move some items into the property's garage the night before or a couple of days before the lease date – DO NOT DO IT!

If you do feel compelled to allow a tenant early access, change the start date of the lease agreement (even if you don't charge rent for additional days). Doing this will protect you and the tenant if something should go wrong. And, of course, you should never permit it unless you have collected all of the move-in monies upfront via certified funds.

Filling a Vacancy

New or first-time landlords often purchase properties that are not suitable as a good rental. After the rehab process, they find themselves with a property that is difficult to rent because of its location, or their mortgage payment is higher than the rents they can collect in that area!

Landlords need to ensure they can list a rental for an amount high enough to cover their mortgage, taxes, and insurance in the area in which the property is located.

Friends and Family

To prevent potential problems with tenants, avoid renting to friends and family members. I know many of you may disagree with me, but I have found that when you put these groups together, all is good—until it is not. If you rent to a family member who loses their job and is unable to pay rent, you will find yourself in a difficult situation. You don't want to find yourself having to make a business decision to evict your family member or friend.

Written Policies and Procedures

Addendum A: This was by far the greatest "tool" I created during my days as a Property Manager. Early in my property management career, I discovered that shortly after move-in, I would get calls or emails from tenants and/or the tenant's agent asking me the same questions over and over. It seemed like there was a lot of confusion and misunderstanding about:

> Where to pay rent

> How to request repairs

> What constituted a repair vs. tenant responsibility

> When and how to give move-out notice

> General questions about the common upkeep of the property, such as changing out smoke detector batteries, lightbulbs, and A/C filters

What seemed to be lacking was a clear and concise instrument (besides the lease agreement) that addressed common questions that tenants could easily refer to. As a landlord, you need to ensure your tenants understand how and where to pay rent. How will you be profitable if you are not collecting rent from a tenant?

Controlling Income and Expenses

A profitable landlord has two basic principles: Control over Income and Expenses

As a property manager, my standard answer to these questions and inquiries was to refer the tenant/agent back to the lease agreement. After all, the tenant had signed, initialed, and dated it to acknowledge the terms and conditions they leased the property under – and their signature was also an acknowledgement they received a copy of the lease agreement, so what could be the issue?

The issue was the lease agreement is 14-16 pages long, and some of the language (as written by an attorney) was a bit confusing or hard to understand.

I thought I was "helping" the tenants by referring them back to the lease agreement and having consistent answers to their questions. But when I realized I was continually being asked the same questions from multiple tenants, I knew that referring the tenant back to their lease was not giving them the information they needed.

When tenants lack a clear understanding of where, how, and to whom rent is paid OR how/when to request repairs, the landlord's profitability will be affected.

One day, I listed all of the questions I was being asked repeatedly and went through the lease agreement line by line to find the answers. I created **Addendum A**, which lists the terms and conditions of the lease agreement in simple to understand language and is attached to each lease agreement.

During tenant orientation, I review Addendum A with each tenant. I've found that by spending 15 minutes to review this shortened version of the lease agreement terms and put the focus on the top questions/inquiries, I freed up more of my time.

Over the years, I have revised and added some information, especially on the return of security deposits.

Addendum A does not replace the lease agreement but becomes a part of the overall lease terms. I have shared this document with other property managers locally and nationally.

For my readers, I have included a link to download Addendum A at the end of this chapter!

Developing a Relationship with your Tenants

In the case study at the beginning of this chapter, I mentioned that when you have long-term tenants, you will probably get to know their families – see their children grow, hear about their accomplishments and defeats. It is part of the relationships of landlords and tenants.

As a landlord, you should consider the following when developing a relationship with your tenants:

PROFESSIONALISM

Respond to any requests from your tenants (repairs or otherwise) in a calm and businesslike manner, even if they are not paying rent, keep asking for trite repairs, or call you at all times day or night. You, as the landlord, are responsible for setting the boundaries with your tenants. Remember, this is your business, and you should conduct yourself as if you were in the office.

COURTESY

You may own the property, but this is the tenant's home. Consider your tenant's needs when the A/C is not working, the hot water tank exploded, or they need clarification on how to work something in the home.

RESPECT

Unless it is a real emergency, do not drop by the property unannounced. If you need to enter the property, make arrangements with your tenant. I was working with a new investor who wanted to offer cleaning services to their tenant so that they could routinely be in the house and check up on the tenant's cleanliness – BIG NO, NO! Do your due diligence upfront, and you won't need to "check-up" on your tenants.

SET BOUNDARIES

Use Addendum A or another written policy or procedure that clearly defines a tenant's responsibility beyond paying rent. Set expectations at the time you sign the lease agreement AND always have in writing what both parties have agreed to, and sign and date this document. When there is a disagreement (and there eventually will be), it makes enforcement of a breach of lease easier to correct if both parties have mutually agreed in writing.

Profitable Tenants During a Pandemic

While this book was being written, our country faced the COVID pandemic, which had an impact on the real estate market and real estate investing in general. During this time, many investors who had only been investing for a couple of years, came out with a "training" program. Their businesses had been hit hard. Foreclosure forbearance and eviction moratoriums were issued, so many real estate investors who focused on buying foreclosures found their well of opportunity drying up, or at the very least, stalled. Landlords, including myself, had to redefine a profitable tenant and what that meant to our business when vacancies did and will occur.

A long-time tenant gave notice mid-pandemic and moved to another country (they had been planning for over a year to move to Spain, so they moved once travel bans were lifted). After the make-ready was completed and the property back on the market, I faced a waiting game. This type of property was normally a quick turn-around to fill a vacancy, and I was surprised it did not rent right away.

But what really made me sit up and take notice was the type of tenant applying for the property. I was getting a steady stream of applicants that were in some phase of the eviction process. The property was in Dallas county, and if you are familiar with the Dallas country politics, you'd know there was no way any landlord was going to eviction court anytime soon!

My tenant selection criteria helps me avoid accepting applicants with an eviction on their record. Many of these applicants did not yet have an eviction yet; it was just filed and waiting in the courts.

My thoughts turned to the tenants getting evicted during the pandemic. If they were being evicted for non-payment due to a job loss through no fault of their own, does that make them "not" a profitable tenant? Well, yes and no! Let me explain. At the beginning of the Pandemic, government relief packages were available to help families pay their rent, but the tenant had to apply to receive the funds. If the tenant applied and did not receive the funds in time (a huge problem for many people in Texas with both unemployment benefits and stimulus checks), so checks were delayed or not received, and the burden fell on the landlords!

We still had to pay our mortgages. Yes, you could call your bank and get a deferral, but the bottom line is there was no assistance for landlords at the time of this writing. So, a pandemic can be one of those situations that is out of your control and prevents you from being a profitable landlord because to be a profitable landlord, rent must be collected.

It is/was quite a frustrating time for landlords during the pandemic. Fortunately, except for our vacancy, all of our tenants continued to pay rent because most were employed as "essential workers" and did not face job layoffs.

UPDATE: During the editing phase of the book, my last rental under COVID has been leased to a very qualified applicant. I am attributing the 45 days on market it took to lease the property that normally leases under a week to our current pandemic circumstances. It illustrates that the market is impacted and shifts both from a culture and business standpoint, and either of these areas can impact a real estate investor's profitability.

Key Takeaways

Profitable landlords will consistently:

❖ Set expectations with their tenants up front

❖ Have a clear set of protocols for paying rent and requesting repairs

❖ Develop a professional and respectful relationships to minimize financial risk and maximize property value

❖ Put everything in writing

CASE STUDY: Know When to Pivot

During the time I was writing this book, our country was facing unprecedented circumstances. The COVID-19 pandemic forced many of us to shelter in place and re-think how we function day-to-day. The official shut down for my area was ordered at the beginning of March 2020. My husband, Brian, and I had been re-evaluating one of our rental properties, considering moving from a single-family rental to an Airbnb – something we wanted to explore.

We researched the area and noted the current number of hotels and Airbnb properties nearby. A waterpark was located within walking distance (two blocks), and we realized we could potentially be sitting on a goldmine. The area had seen tremendous tourism growth since we purchased the property in 2016.

So, as good landlords, we contacted our tenant, whose lease was ending, and gave her notice to vacate the premises. Our plan was simple—have the tenant move out by the end of March. We could then renovate and furnish the property for a suitable Airbnb and have it available to lease by May 1, 2020.

Fast forward to COVID. At first, we thought as most people did, this is temporary, we will see how it shakes out. Our tenant had not secured a new rental, so because of the market, we extended her lease another 30 days (yes, we got all of this in writing!). We figured if the property was ready by June 1, we would still benefit from the tourism business when the amusement park opened.

But the governor ordered a lockdown, and the water park would not be opening any time soon.

So, what is a property owner to do? We revisited our game plan and determined it would not be profitable to have a great-paying tenant move out and leave the property vacant for a month or two while renovating the property.

It is important to note that we had an excellent tenant in our property who paid rent on time AND took care of the property. However, the rent was just a bit under what we needed for this rental to be profitable. The previous year, we increased the rent, and the tenant communicated to us that they were on a fixed income, and that was the maximum rent they could pay.

Due to increases in property taxes, we had to raise the rent by $100 per month. The tenant was not looking forward to moving and realized quickly after viewing other houses that our property was very affordable for the area. The tenant agreed to the higher rent, and we executed a 12-month renewal—this was a win-win. As landlords, we retained a "profitable tenant" AND continued to increase our cash flow on this rental property.

The biggest takeaway from this story: as a profitable landlord, you have to be flexible, and need to have enough room in your portfolios to make "business" decisions that correlate with your financial goals. Yes, we liked the tenant, but being a profitable landlord means making business decisions aligned with your financial goals.

Have you struggled to find the right tenant for your property? Are you spending more time "showing" your property that you want to? We want to help you to save time, money, and energy when working with potential tenants.

Visit the link below to download our *Tenant Criteria Checklist, Four Key Questions to ask Potential Tenants*, AND *Tenant Move-In Checklist*.

https://mailchi.mp/kbnhomes.com/qtnb5c13oe

Finding Profitable Tenants with the Profitable Landlord System

I detail how to find, screen, and manage your tenant application process in the *Profitable Landlord System*. I caution you not to rush this process. Take your time screening potential renters to save you time and money down the line.

ProfitableLandlordSystem.com

CHAPTER 3:
BUYING PROPERTIES

By now, you know that I like to ask questions. If you are a real estate investor, you probably find yourself asking the same three questions repeatedly:

1. What should we buy?

2. When should we buy it?

3. How should we buy it?

These three questions could apply to almost any business. Do you know what questions you should be asking? If not, how do you find the questions to ask (property size, location, etc.)?

In this chapter, we will focus on "How should we buy it?"

Traditional Lenders

You can't rely on one of the "Big 4's" to be your go-to lender when buying investment properties. Chase, Wells Fargo, Bank of America, and Citibank do not offer the lending products needed to build a large portfolio of rental properties. When we first started buying single-family properties, it was easy to get a loan on a rental property.

We tried to purchase our first rental property through Chase bank. After weeks of providing every required financial document (tax returns, pay stubs, HOA statements, utility bills, etc.), they could not make the lending deal happen despite the fact that we had outstanding credit, a large down payment, and low debt-to-income ratio. The property we were purchasing required repairs, and Chase would not lend on it until the repairs were made.

Since then, we have learned a lot about lenders and found the key is to make ourselves and the investment as risk-free as possible to the lender. We create a business plan for each property we want to purchase and present it to the lender with details about the asset's appreciation once the repairs are complete. This formula works great for the lender and us. Now we have a resource of lenders that know we provide value to their lending portfolio, and they provide value to us by enabling us to continue to purchase properties. This relationship has been vital to our ongoing success as profitable landlords.

If you are buying your first rental property, you *may* be able to get it financed with a traditional/conventional loan. When we purchased our first rental property, it was much easier to get financing from traditional lenders than it is today. If you could breathe, you could get a mortgage. Countrywide Home Loans funded our first rental property. Of course, that was before the 2008 housing market crash. Like other industries, the mortgage and lending institutions are always in flux.

Buying our first few rental properties was relatively easy. At the time, money was easy to get, and you could finance rental properties with as little as 10% down. We were able to buy some rental properties with an 80/10/10, which is basically two mortgages (80% for the first mortgage, 10% for the second mortgage, and a 10% down payment).

We are debt averse. Having mortgages on our rental properties is good debt, and we put down about 20% on each property we purchased to ensure we had some equity. But after doing that a few times, we ran out of money. I have learned over the years that I need to use other's people money (OPM). The "cost" of borrowing money is worth the investment in the long run.

Asset-Based Lenders

How did we transition from conventional loans? We were forced to find other options because we no longer qualified for conventional loans due to the number of rental properties we owned. **So, I started asking questions!!!** My investor friends and mentors were hush-hush about it, but I eventually learned about Asset-Based Lenders.

In asset-based lending, the focus is on the feasibility of the deal to make a profit. Most asset-based lenders understand real estate investing and can recognize a good deal. Because this is relationship-based lending, I have built a large network of private money lenders and maintain a good reputation as a real estate investor. Working with my private network enables me to negotiate better terms and lower interest rates.

I have used traditional lenders, hard money lenders, asset-based lenders, and private money lenders over the years. I continuously add to my list of lender contacts because the lenders are fluid and change as your business changes.

CASE STUDY – ASSET-BASED LOANS

We found our first asset-based lender through a mutual friend who was an investor with a large real estate brokerage. She had taken me under her wing to mentor me on real estate investing. One day, the president of a lending institution came to our office to meet with my mentor. She was running late for the meeting, so I started talking to him about my investing goals. At the time, I had a rental property under contract, and I was trying to figure out a way to get the money to buy it!

The lender suggested I complete a financial statement and apply for the proceeds for the loan. My husband and I had great credit, our debt-to-income ratio was well within the acceptable range, and we had cashflow on our other rental properties. We had been investing in single-family rental properties for about 24 months.

The lender did his due diligence and checked my references. He called my friend/mentor and asked if she would lend money to me and if I was trustworthy. Without the great relationship I had with my mentor, we would not have been approved for the financing. I was able to continue to grow my wealth and continue my journey to build my legacy.

Fast forward a few years, our rental portfolio had increased significantly, and we were self-funding some of our deals. We wanted to refinance the current mortgage on one property and pull out our equity to fund another deal. First, we approached our current lender; however, they were unwilling to do a cash out re-fi. We didn't let that stop us and continued to ask questions until we found another lender who was willing to do a cash out re-fi. The interest rate was lower, which in turn reduced our monthly payment. Not only did we put some tax-free money in our pocket to buy more rental properties, we increased our monthly cash flow.

MONEY MINDSET

If you are reading this or, better yet, are a student of the Profitable Landlord System, you are more than likely looking for a way to quit your day job, get out of debt, and have the financial means to have that life you want. Before creating the Profitable Landlord System, I asked more than 100 real estate investor landlords why they do what they do. Their top answers:

➢ Retire Early
➢ Financial Freedom
➢ Quit a 9-to-5 job
➢ Get out of debt

Every new real estate investor I start working with tells me they need money to get started in real estate, so their first go-to investment strategy is *wholesaling*. I have wholesaled a few properties in my day and know that wholesaling is really hard work. You need excellent negotiation skills, which few newbie investors have. You must negotiate a low purchase price with a seller so that you can sell it at a higher price. If it is a good deal, then keep it for yourself and find a way to pay for it. There are many ways to fund real estate deals, and I recommend new investors spend their time building a network of lenders first. If you have a deal, you can find the money to fund it!

In the Profitable Landlord System, we identify risk factors to determine if the property is a good deal. We also teach you how to "reduce" your risk to a lender when looking for money. A lender is looking for a risk-free investment. They want the borrower to have skin in the game, either through equity in the property or a sizable down payment. To find a profitable lender, you (as the borrower) need to demonstrate the following:

➤ Knowledge of real estate investing

➤ Reputation

➤ Ability to pay (lenders want to know how you will pay them back)

➤ Network

Notice I didn't include cash on hand in that list. Although I believe a profitable landlord should have a cushion for repairs, emergencies, etc.

It is possible to buy rental properties if you have bad credit, no credit, or very little money for a down payment. The process may be more difficult, but it can be done if someone is guiding you.

I had to get my mind right about money. Real estate investing involves large amounts of money, and if you are like us when we started, you do not have "extra" money. Our mentor helped us learn how to avoid big financial mistakes in real estate investing to become profitable landlords. Yes, we made mistakes (and you will, too), but nothing catastrophic that caused us to go bankrupt or lose any of our properties.

It's important to have a good mindset about money! People have a lot of "feelings" about money. As cliché as it sounds, you need to spend money (buy properties) to make money. Our step-by-step training manual will give you facts to help you make the right decision!

MY DECLARATION ABOUT MONEY

When I created my Life Vision (where I want to go in my journey), I was trying to achieve:

- ➢ Financial freedom
- ➢ Valuable resource to clients
- ➢ Ability to take care of family
- ➢ Peaceful, low-level stress day-to-day life
- ➢ Enjoyment in each day as it unfolds
- ➢ Satisfaction in what we do - work doesn't feel like work
- ➢ A unique and significant office
- ➢ Confidence about life

DECLARATION OF NEW EMPOWERING BELIEF

*I authorize the Perfect Mindset about
Money and Money in my Life!*

This is my one thought: *I am good enough; money neither defines me nor has any power over me. Money is only energy, waiting for an opportunity. I have the freedom to choose how much money I have.*

I know that:

> ➢ I have enough money

> ➢ I have always had enough money

> ➢ I have ability to make money anytime, anywhere

Recognizing these facts caused me to change my thinking and begin to heal from toxic limiting beliefs. No guilt, fear, or belief in my conscious mind can interrupt or affect this new mindset. I am moved into a powerful state of being by consciously making the decision and declaration that I have enough money, and there has always been enough money.

From this declaration forward, I cast in motion powerful forces of healing in my mind that restore me to my true reality, and I am backed by evidence from a series of events that have unfolded right before me.

I have a healthy mind and body and am ready to experience everything in life. I believe in goodness and fresh flowing ideas. I expect the right things to happen, and when they do not, I will not be dismayed or let that prevent me from staying in a Powerful State of Being. I am meant to do great things, grow as much wealth as I desire, and have the life I have always wanted, and the money will flow to make that happen.

My imagination is a powerful force for creating good. The power of my imagination is tremendous. As I use it, I expand my consciousness of well-being and feel secure about where I am in life, spiritually and financially. I will use my imagination to quell those limiting beliefs and promote my new belief that I have always had enough money and will continue to stack evidence until this new belief is part of my psyche and being. My subconscious mind welcomes this new picture. Holding this vision for a few seconds has great therapeutic power. With it, I am immediately directing my subconscious towards creative action. No fears, doubts, or limiting beliefs can interfere with this image, the image of how God sees me, the image of who I truly am. Doing this once or twice a day has a powerful effect and adds even more power to my decision to be healthy.

I see myself as being carefree and having energy flow through me with new ideas that will lead to having more money. I am not stuck on a dollar amount, as I know that there will always be enough, and there always has been enough. And that my being and worth are not measured by a dollar amount. To have enough for what I need now is all I ever need.

I am planning, brainstorming, and letting go of untrue beliefs about money. I do not feel less than just because my bank account is not as large as someone else's. I have value-added ideas and can contribute to a bigger picture and have an impact in and on the world through my creative process.

I am feeling more and more at peace with my new belief. I am sleeping better, I am not fretting or needlessly worrying about something that is not true. I do not need to worry about money anymore, as there has always been enough, and there will always be enough. I have always had the ability to make as much money as I want. I choose not to focus on how much money I have or want, I will focus on energy that brings money in, and let that energy guide the money flow. The energy I provide and put into universe will be enough to generate however much money I need, want, or desire.

If you suffer from a mindset that prohibits you from moving forward, I encourage to participate in the above exercise. Write out a declaration about a limiting belief you have about yourself. By writing it down, the power that the limiting belief has over you will start to diminish.

You can control the role money plays in your life and real estate investing. If you adopt the mindset that money is a tool that can help, you will have:

➢ More money – I believe you make more money with money

➢ Peace of mind – Don't think that you don't have enough or that money defines you

➢ Ability to have the life you always wanted – Using money as a tool is just one way to increase your net worth.

If you think of the questions you need to ask and use money as a tool to help in your real estate investing career, then you have already started to change your mind set about your journey as a real estate investor. Download the *Mindset Declaration Form* and some sample questions I ask my profitable lenders at the link below:

Key Takeaways

❖ Know the differences between traditional lending and asset-based lending.

❖ Position yourself and the property as a low risk to the lender.

❖ Have a business plan to present to the lender.

❖ Do not take no for an answer. If one lender can't do it, go to the next lender.

Finding Profitable Funders with The Profitable Landlord System

The Profitable Landlord System was built on asking the right questions. Each question posed in the system was a question we were asked on our real estate journey, and we tested those questions with each rental property we added to our portfolio.

Whether you invest in the stock market, are a private money lender, or are trying to find the right tenant for your properties, not only do you have to ask questions – **YOU MUST KNOW THE RIGHT QUESTIONS TO ASK!**

---

https://mailchi.mp/kbnhomes.com/qtnb5c13oe

CHAPTER 4:
USING PROFITABLE MANAGERS

Property Management is near and dear to my heart. I have been in property management for over a decade and managed more than 1000 doors. I learned a lot about myself, honed my people skills, and had a good time doing it! I got into property management because I wanted to know more about being a landlord and what it takes to make money investing in single-family homes.

I have learned you can have the best deal, location, and mortgage for your investment, but if you make mistakes when selecting and managing your rental properties, you will see your profits go to the wayside.

Now, don't get me wrong. A profitable landlord can and should manage their properties when they first start investing IF they have the time and organizational skills required. If you are short on time, unorganized, or too friendly, you need to hire a property manager.

A good property will make you profitable as long as you save time, energy, and money (STEM). The fee you pay each month to a property manager is minuscule compared to the time and energy a property manager can save you.

CASE STUDY – PROPERTY MANAGEMENT

I worked with an investor who had spent a great deal of time and energy to lease just one property. He lived about 45 minutes away from his rental property, and he didn't want to hire a property management company and pay the leasing fee (generally equal to one month's rent).

The landlord listed his property and made 1-2 trips per day for 14 days to show it to prospective tenants. He put approximately 800 miles on his car and spent 21 hours driving back and forth — and did not find a tenant.

He was referred to me to help lease and manage the property. Using our network and resources, we had the property leased within three days of signing him up, and the new tenant moved in the following week.

Key Takeaways

❖ We saved him time – he no longer had to drive to show his property (21 hours is a lot of wasted energy to be sitting in a car)

❖ We saved him money – the property was not sitting vacant with no rent coming in

❖ We saved him energy – He did not have to rush to the property each time a showing was scheduled

❖ He could now focus on finding other properties because he was no longer concentrating on leasing just one property!

SELF-MANAGING PROPERTIES

I was one of very few real estate brokers in Texas certified to teach other property managers how to manage properties. When I left my property management career behind, it was hard for me to let another property manager take over my rental portfolio.

I am a bit of a control freak, so that was one issue. But more importantly, each property management company I interviewed could not answer my questions, didn't track the KPIs necessary to determine if you are a profitable landlord, and didn't answer their phones. If they aren't answering their phones when a potential new client calls, I had to wonder if they would answer for my tenants!

I was slow to pull the trigger on this one aspect of being a profitable landlord. I had self-managed for so long and had a really good, automated system in place for my tenants. Many of the tenants had been in place for a long time, so the management side was relatively easy for me. I also knew exactly how to manage my properties, minimize repair costs, and maximize rent collections.

If you are self-managing your properties and continue to make a profit, that is great! But I encourage you to put it on paper to determine how much time, energy, and money it costs to self-manage your properties. Many new investors are not equipped to handle all of the issues that come up with tenants. Their mindset is to "save" money instead of visualizing how hiring the right property manager will get them closer to their financial goals.

FINDING THE RIGHT PROPERTY MANAGER

Property managers are not alike, and this is another area that requires due diligence and an understanding of what a profitable property manager should be doing for their landlords.

1. Are you asking all the right questions?

2. Do you know what to ask?

3. What KPIs does the property management company use to track performance?

4. When are owners paid? HUGE red flag if you get different answers here

5. What is the Eviction Ratio? This is the number one rating I use for evaluating a profitable property manager

When I meet new realtors or new real estate investors, I hear a lot of enthusiasm to become property managers. They think it is easy money – basically, sit back and collect the rent, collect your fee, and repeat each month. I have met property managers who charge a flat fee of $50.00 regardless of the property location, condition, or amount of rent collected. Their philosophy is quantity over quality. That property management company grew to 150 doors because they attracted owners who liked the $50 per month flat fee. Guess what? You get what you pay for, and that property management company went out of business as fast as they grew.

Skills Needed for Property Managers

Property management is not for the faint of heart. There are specific skills a profitable property manager must possess:

1. Organization: Track lease terms, send renewals and other time-sensitive notices. Coordinate with vendors and tenants, and follow up to make sure any repairs are complete, and the vendor is paid

2. Time Management: Maintenance and repair requests should be handled in a timely manner.

3. People: Interact with property owners, realtors, vendors, applicants and their families

4. Negotiation: Negotiate lease terms and rental rates, repair costs, tenant disputes, possible eviction scenarios, and build a successful property management business.

Property managers should also be knowledge about restrictions, regulations, and covenants that impact the properties they manage.

As you can see, a property management company does a lot more than collect rent. When it is time for you to hire a management company, consider all necessary criteria and don't make a decision based on price alone.

PROPERTY MANAGEMENT MINDSET

Your mindset about property management and how it can make you a profitable landlord will shift when you:

➢ See your time as having a monetary value – paying a property manager gives you back time and money

➢ See your energy as preserved and can channel your energy into other areas of your real estate investing

➢ Change your thinking about money – paying a property manager gives you more freedom, which allows you to focus on your financial goals

➢ Documentation – A property lease can be over 20 pages, plus all of the addendums that cover every situation and are designed to protect owners and tenants – how will you stay updated?

Visit the site below to download my top questions to ask potential property managers and start interviewing them today!

https://mailchi.mp/kbnhomes.com/qtnb5c13oe

Finding Profitable Managers with The Profitable Landlord System

A Profitable Manager will manage your properties with detail to cash flow, vacancy rates, and repair costs. They will also enhance the overall appreciation of your property and keep the property rented with profitable tenants. Profitable Managers can be found through professional property management associations, realtor referrals, and investor networking.

Key Takeaways

❖ Hiring the right property manager will save you time, money, and energy (STEM)

❖ Ask the right questions to hire the right property manager

Chapter 5:
Building Our Profitable Team

If you are ready to expand, scale, and start the growth process so you can eventually step away to have the life you dream of, congratulations! But wait, there are some steps you must take and questions you must ask yourself before bringing on a team of individuals to avoid a decline in your profitability.

Most entrepreneurs are used to being in charge and tend to be control freaks, but that makes them successful. The drive to get it done and get it done now is often accompanied with the mindset that no one can do it better, faster, or more efficiently. So, you must let go of this mindset!

Building Your Team

Building a team can be a rewarding experience or your worst nightmare! If you have an entrepreneurial spirit, it can challenge you to the bone. Most of us hang onto some control of our business and, let's face it, we are hard pressed to find someone else who can do it better than we do. I struggled with this, and I am guessing you may also. It was a hard lesson to learn, and what I can share with you is If you don't learn the art of letting go, it will be impossible or downright nerve-wracking to have a profitable team.

How I built my team

Write it out

> ➢ My goals – where I wanted to go

> ➢ My processes – how was I going to get there

> ➢ My daily planner – schedule the time to do it

I am old school when it comes to list writing. Even with all of the electronic gadgets available to keep track of lists, calendars, etc., I still work best when I handwrite my "to-do" lists every day. I keep a small notebook with tear out pages. I put the date at the top of the list, and write down everything I need to accomplish, books I want to read, or even my follow-up calls. When I complete a task, I cross it off the list. For me, this system works twofold:

1. Sense of accomplishment at the end of the day when I see how many "to dos" I completed.

2. Constant reminder to stay focused and on track to achieve my daily, weekly, and monthly goals.

During my career, I have had multiple opportunities to grow a profitable team. Whether you are collecting blood donations OR collecting rental properties, the fundamentals of growing a successful and profitable team remain the same.

Listed below are the top four reasons profitable teams succeed:

1. **Leadership**. There is a clear vision and mission about where the leader wants to go, the main focus, and what needs to be accomplished.

2. **Clear Goals and Objectives**. Measured KPIs to determine if the goals are being met, how it is measured, and who is measuring.

3. **Written Procedures and Instructions**. Who is doing what and when is it being done? This is the hardest part for most people, as they have "just" been doing it and what they know is in their head. All leaders must take time write out procedures and instructions.

Tip: I write a job aide for each specific task that needs to be accomplished. Then, I give it to one of my staff and tell them to follow what is says. If I have written the job aide correctly, they will complete the task. If they get stuck, I know I left out a step. This has worked for me in every situation when I hire someone to complete a task/ job without fail.

4. **Focus and Ability to Stay on Task**. Pay attention to what you really want to accomplish. In real estate investing, there are many moving parts:

    i.   Marketing

    ii.   Deal Analysis

    iii.   Funding the Deal

    iv.   Strategy

    v.   Closing

Within those moving parts, a real estate investor can get lost in the small things that need to be done so that the deal does not fall through the cracks. As you become more profitable in your real estate business, you will find you have less and less time to handle all the facets of these five areas by yourself.

Focus and Automation

We all should be paying attention to the financial part of our businesses, but as you grow, your time and focus are pulled, so you need a profitable team so you can focus on growth instead of one task, goal, or objective.

Automation allows you to grow your business while not wasting time doing repetitive tasks; it gives you some breathing room to look at your overall objective and what is needed to move to the next level. For example, by automating your marketing, you will increase your deal flow. When deal flow increases, all areas of your business will grow, and you will need to be prepared to handle the influx of deals, find the money to fund the deals, and allow time to analyze and determine exit strategies for each of the deals.

Before you grow your deal flow, which is what we all want, take the time to write out your procedures, even if you just stick them in a folder or store them in your computer. When it is time to take the next steps necessary for growth, you already have a start on knowing the right people to add to your team.

Be aware of the following issues when growing your team:

1. **Constant Turnover** – you are not matching the right person with the right task. You are hiring because you like the applicant, but they were not capable of doing the job.

2. **Constant Training** – your outline of the duties required is not clear or easy to follow. Your hires are confused, make mistakes, or the job just does not get done.

3. **Not Achieving Your Goals/Objectives** – your team is unaware of the goals/objectives or the mission/vision is not clear. You have not defined and tracked the right KPIs.

Bottom Line: YOU and only YOU are responsible for your profitable team. It is a huge undertaking, and I urge you to prepare before you get to this level. As you are reading this chapter, put the book down for 10 minutes and quickly write out why you do what you do and what you want to accomplish.

As I said before, when I interviewed 100 landlords, they told me the reason they wanted to be a landlord was:

1. Quit the 9-to-5 Job and Retire Early

2. Financial Freedom

3. Generational Wealth

It takes time, planning, and organization to be a profitable landlord. In the step-by-step Profitable Landlord System, I include my planning tools that helped me get where I am at today.

Planning is the key to growth. Yes, some people get by through the seat of their pants, but when the market shifts, will they have the systems in place to weather any storm? Maybe yes, maybe no. My strategy has served my family well. We paid attention to the markets, decided when to buy and hold, when to flip, and how to monetize each lead that came our way.

Real estate investing became the vehicle for myself and my family to create a life we want and deserve. You can have that type of life as well – you deserve it BUT you must take the steps, the calculated risk and stay focused and organized!

1. THE RIGHT TEAM AND PROCESSES

When adding members to your team, you need to have documented procedures and clearly defined roles.

> *"Make sure you have the right
> person in the right seat."*
>
> – Gino Wickman, author of the book
> "Traction: Get a Grip on your Business"

2. PUT IT IN WRITING.

Don't expect others to know what you have done to grow your business. The number one mistake I see people make is not taking the time to write out their:

1. Mission Statement and Vision
2. Job Descriptions
3. Goals
4. Procedures
5. Follow-up and Evaluations

Most real estate investors focus wholly on closing deals. Deal flow is the life of this business, but you need to carve out some time to set up your processes each day, week, and month to grow and expand your business. Otherwise, your team will be built on a weak foundation that will eventually crumble.

3. HIRING AND ONBOARDING

If you are a solo entrepreneur, there is a high probability that you work with one or more family members. My husband, daughter, and soon-to-be son-in-law all have a part in our real estate company, but sometimes the lines get blurred because we are family.

Personality is key to a profitable team – not only amongst the team members, but also with sellers, tenants, and other real estate investors. Abrasive personalities will not go far, and you won't be able to slip away to your beach house if Aunt Sally has a history of treating your tenants poorly.

Additionally, new team members must be adequately trained on all tasks. Establish checks and balances and develop mechanisms to measure results to ensure your team remains profitable when you step away from the day-to-day activities.

Case Study

We are a family business; my daughter is the marketing/ social media manager, and my husband is the IT director. Our son-in-law is new to real estate investing, so he is my sounding board when I roll out a new program, marketing campaign, or webinar. If he understands what I am teaching, I know I am creating a user-friendly course.

I wanted to add a bookkeeper to the team, but I wasn't really sure what I needed. I had always handled the financial tasks for our business, but I was doing more speaking engagements, and my time was limited for this very important aspect of our business. I already had a CPA in place, so I thought I could hire an assistant to handle the entries, track the receipts, filing, and other general office activities.

I hired someone who was good at what she did, but she was not a bookkeeper. When doing my taxes that year, I discovered she had made a $60,000 error by duplicating transactions in QuickBooks. It took me several hours and multiple phone calls with my CPA to figure out where the mistake was

What went wrong? I did not hire the right person for the right seat. I needed someone that under-stood basic accounting because I do not. I got it all straightened out, hired a bookkeeper, and assigned the person to other daily tasks more suited to her skill set.

Although that mistake was resolved relatively quickly, it distracted me from growing my business. I had to stop what I was doing, fix the current issues, evaluate what went wrong, and correct the hiring/onboarding procedures.

Mindset and Profitable Teams

Some changes that you will need to focus on:

➢ Delegating – even if you can do it all, you shouldn't

➢ Document all processes

➢ Create a Vision

➢ Share your Vision

➢ Celebrate milestones

➢ Measure and track your performance

Key Performance Indicators (KPIs)

Building a profitable team is a great way to scale, but you need to ensure your staff are properly trained and understand your mission. Develop KPIs to track performances and ensure you remain a profitable landlord.

In my previous career, I managed blood bank call centers. We had a huge turnover and were in constant training mode. I decided we needed some training tools that were easy to follow, simple to use, and repeatable without requiring much effort from my management team. These job aides may be useful in your business during onboarding and staff training. Click on the link below to download two job aides I wrote, implemented, and now use in my real estate business:

Building Profitable Teams with The Profitable Landlord System

A Profitable Team has built relationships with your Profitable Tenants, Funders, and Managers. The Profitable Team has a high level of retention, has developed a database of contacts, documented processes (*when this happens, then do that*), and has clearly defined roles

Key Takeaways:

❖ Set goals

❖ Get everything in writing

❖ Be consistent in your activities

❖ Follow-up, measure, and track your results

https://mailchi.mp/kbnhomes.com/qtnb5c13oe

CHAPTER 6:
CREATING OUR PROFITABLE PLAN

No matter where you are in life, chances are you did some planning to get there. Taking a road trip requires you to plan which route you will take and where to eat and sleep. When hiring a babysitter, you look for reliability, references, and cost. Most things in life take planning, and being a profitable landlord is no exception. I would make the case that more planning is needed to ensure you:

➢ Achieve your financial goals

➢ Minimize financial risk

➢ Are rewarded with success

➢ Create the life you desire

Getting Started

The number one question I hear from new real estate investors is: **WHERE DO I START?**

There is so much information about real estate investing – books, webinars, podcasts, real estate groups, and your cousin! It's a wonder anyone gets started after trying to sift through the training.

To be a real estate investor, at some point, you have to stop reading books, step away from your computer, attend fewer networking events, AND jump in! If you are stuck, you need to find a trusted, seasoned investor who will mentor you.

Be willing to pay for that mentoring and coaching — you need to have a stake in the game. Don't think that learning how to wholesale properties for quick cash will enable you to create wealth.

Every successful real estate investor I know attributes their success to two things:

1. Having a trusted mentor/coach

2. Having a system to follow and be accountable

That's all it takes to get started. You don't have to know every step of the process; you need to put your efforts into finding someone to work with who is successful, has a track record, and, most importantly, is aligned with your goals and aspirations. You are looking for someone you like, know, and trust.

In the Profitable Landlord System, we outline how to set up your real estate business, from the basics such as your name, to how many leads you need to generate your take-home pay. In other words, we will walk you through how to set up your Profitable Planner!

Have you thought about your take-home pay lately? Are you diligent about tracking your expenses each month? If not, we have a simple tool that you can use to start you on this journey.

Planning is key to:

➢   Quitting the 9 to 5 job – you need to know how much income to replace

> ➤ Early retirement – how many rental properties will that require

> ➤ Create generational wealth – set your Profit Risk Indicator (PRI) for your rental portfolio

I created these tools for our business. We had to know where we wanted to go and how to get there, and the tools available in the Profitable Landlord System guided us on our journey while keeping us on track to achieve our success.

Once you have established where you want to be in the next 12 months to five years, it is easier to set the goals and use an accountability tool such as a Profitable Planner. Over the years, we determined which Key Indicators at a glance would tell us if we were staying the course, or if we needed to alter some aspect of our business, such as tenant turnover, increased property taxes, or emergency repairs.

PLANNER DEVELOPMENT PROCESS

1. Establish Your Gap – Where you are and where you are relative to where we want to be

2. Create an Accountability Chart – Establish daily, weekly, monthly, quarterly, and yearly routines to monitor goals

3. Identify the Most Profitable Activities

4. Scheduled Activities for Consistency

5. Executed and Revised – Measure what is working, what is not

By incorporating a routine, we were able to assign marketing campaigns and activities and created our deal flow of profitable sellers. A detailed marketing plan for daily, weekly, and monthly activities kept us on track to reach our financial goals. Without our profitable planner, we would not have been able to scale our business.

CELEBRATE THE SMALL STUFF

We also incorporated celebrations at different milestones. When we found something was working, we would celebrate the process and results. This helps to reinforce your mindset to continue to work on being consistent. Often, when we have some success, we stop our day-to-day routine that led to the success, have a dip in our business, and wonder why. This can lead to a negative mindset that the process is not working.

Take time to celebrate your wins, no matter how small. A solo entrepreneur can feel lonely at times without the opportunity to share their successes. If you are comfortable with social media, blast it out there. I typically reach out to another real estate investor so we can pump each other up!!!

If you want to learn more about the Profitable Landlord Planner, visit the site below to download the worksheet to determine how much you want to earn from your real estate business.

Key Takeaways

- ❖ When you plan, you succeed

- ❖ Successful real estate investors invest in themselves for coaching and accountability

https://mailchi.mp/kbnhomes.com/qtnb5c13oe

Chapter 7:
Our Legacy

If you have enjoyed reading this book, I hope you will share it with your family and friends. Brian and I enjoyed putting our thinking caps on and creating the Profitable Landlord System. As I said in the beginning, we had a great mentor who not only showed us the ropes and started our journey as real estate investors but was also a good friend. She and I shared a property management company, and it was fun and exciting. In ten years, not a day went by that we did not comment, complain, and chuckle about life as a property manager.

She passed away unexpectantly, and I was left with a massive hole in my heart and my business. Our friendship had grown, blossomed, and deepened over the years. We traveled together, watched our children grow, and talked about the day that we would leave property management behind to hang out on the beach and see our adult children marry and have grandchildren.

She never made it that far. Because her life was cut short, I was propelled to start a new journey on my own as a trusted coach and mentor. I wanted to give back to people who were genuinely interested in becoming real estate investors and set myself apart from every guru, coach, and educator in the real estate space. Giving back and supporting my community is part of a bigger WHY for my family.

In 2018, I wrote *Winning Deals in Heels* to detail my journey and the journey of nine other successful real estate women, who, just like you, had to start somewhere. It is a great read about inspiration, motivation, and finding the self-confidence to succeed as a real estate investor. Part of the proceeds from the sale of the book are donated to Hope's Door, based in Plano, Texas. They are a nonprofit organization that helps families heal from domestic violence. We were fortunate to have Hope's Door sponsor a book signing party when we launched the book.

When Brian and I created the Profitable Landlord System and subsequently wrote this book, we wanted to make sure that an even greater amount of proceeds went to a non-profit near and dear to our hearts: Map of Hope. Brian, my daughter Kelcie, and I founded this non-profit, with the primary purpose to raise awareness about mental health issues and how they affect individuals and their personal and professional relationships.

Our family has dealt with mental health illness, specifically chronic depression. Brian was diagnosed with this debilitating disease when he was in his mid-thirties and is still dealing with it three decades later. A new treatment has given him and our family a new outlook on life.

Donations to Map of Hope help pay for Transcranial Magnetic Stimulation (TMS) treatment, a proven, non-invasive treatment for depression. After years of prescription medicine cocktails, talk, biofeedback, and other types of therapy, our family was introduced to this treatment, which was nothing short of a miracle for Brian.

What does this have to do with real estate investing? Our continued success investing in real estate has given us the time and resources to start a non-profit that has brought meaning to our lives. We want to help other families get to where we have been in the past few years.

Our step-by-step process is simple, repeatable, and predictable, allowing investors to realize their financial goals by using the roadmap and tools provided.

I may have made it seem easy, and for someone who is driven, consistent, and willing to put in the time, real estate investing can be very financially rewarding. The Profitable Landlord System IS NOT a get-rich-quick type of investing. To build wealth and financial freedom, you need:

➢ TIME – for property appreciation, tax advantages, and paying down your mortgage with rental payments from your tenants

➢ CONSISTENCY – you must have continual deal flow through targeted marketing

➢ PERSISTENCE – you will have setbacks and problem tenants – our job is to give you the tools to help you minimize your financial risks

➢ FOLLOW THROUGH – many real estate deals result from follow-up with a seller, referrals, or marketing

Do You Have a Why?

Why do you want (or continue) to be a real estate investor? What do you want to achieve through real estate investing? Do you enjoy being a real estate investor?

I am so passionate about real estate investing; I literally could talk about it all the time. There are so many facets, challenges, and opportunities. Still, you have to be open to exploring. Know your strengths and identify where your skills are lacking and take the appropriate steps to fill in the gaps.

Case Study

I had a prior client who was so shy, and she didn't think she would ever be able to talk with sellers. She was very timid and unsure of what she would say or how she would buy rental properties.

There are many ways to find deals and work on your deal flow, no matter your skillset. We hired a virtual assistant for this client to answer incoming calls and ask a specific set of questions to determine if this was indeed a profitable seller. If a seller met the client's criteria, we would join conference calls with the seller and our client and use pre-written scripts to walk the client step-by-step through the process so she would gain confidence and knowledge.

Within 30 days, our client mustered enough knowledge and confidence to start handling her seller lead calls by herself. She was still timid and continued to make mistakes, but each call brought her closer to the overall goal of working with profitable sellers, and she was able to land her first deal and start her journey as a real estate investor.

This client had:

Desire – She really wanted to learn about real estate investing

Commitment – She was committed to put in the time and do whatever necessary to overcome her areas of weakness

Dedication – She followed through on our step-by-step program and did not allow setbacks to prevent her from achieving her overall goals

Vision – She envisioned her successful real estate journey, and with our guidance, adjusted her mindset

My Goals

My family and I are more than real estate investors. We envision a life of health, abundance, and giving back to our community. Real estate investing allows us to achieve our goals and continue to build our vision of what we want our life to look like. We have setbacks and make mistakes, but we get up, dust ourselves off, evaluate our missteps, and alter our direction to avoid making that mistake again.

I recently experienced a setback that I had not pre-viously encountered. At the onset of the COVID-19 pandemic, right as the country was shut down, we had three properties under contract we were preparing to re-hab. We hired a contractor through our hard money lender who had done the inspections for our repair draws (if you don't know what I am talking about – it's okay, you will learn this in the Profitable Landlord System courses on Profitable Funders!)

My Mistake

I did not do my due diligence on this contractor. Because he was affiliated with the lender who I had known for quite some time, I broke my first rule — ALWAYS get references.

This contractor turned out to be the contractor from hell, and he performed some of the worst work I have ever encountered. He hired sub-contractors to fix the problems that did a worse job than the initial sub-contractor. So, I fired the contractor.

The contractor then went online and filed a "NOTICE OF LIEN." I had never heard of this. When I viewed the actual documents, *This is not a lien* was written at the top of the document. I found out this is a trick that dishonest contractors use to bully an unsuspecting investor into paying for a job that is not complete or completed with poor workmanship. The contractor put this notice TWO of my properties, although he sent me an email that I did not owe any monies for the work on one of the properties.

What I Did Right

❖ Documented the entire project and took LOTS of pictures.

❖ Retained emails, text messages, and third-party documentation of the poor workmanship.

❖ Documented every conversation about the rehab and follow-up required when working with vendors.

I am alerting you about this so you will not be intimidated by shoddy contractors. The most frustrating part of the NOTICE OF LIEN is that it clouds your title. If you attempt to refinance or sell the property, you have to go through the process of getting it removed.

This is an example of a misstep that can happen when you are a real estate investor. You must do your due diligence on the property, tenant, lender, AND contractors without fail, as this can negatively impact your ability to be a profitable landlord.

To remediate this problem, we did the following:

1. Reviewed and documented the scope of work

2. Fired the contractor after giving him an opportunity to correct the workmanship

3. Removed the false lien through proper and legal means

4. Held the contractor accountable for filing a wrongful lien/notice of lien

5. Notified the lender that their inspector was doing sub-par work and was no longer performing inspections, putting the lender at risk as well

6. Ensured the lender took appropriate steps to prevent other investors from having problems with the same contractor

I am happy to report that I was able to successfully remove the notice – although it took a bit of time. Seasoned profitable landlords from time to time will have missteps and make financial mistakes. (I had to hire another contractor to fix the problems of the previous contractor!) We never lost sight of the overall goal. Once we realized our mistake, we immediately took action to remediate.

In closing, if you are ready to

➤ Be PROFITABLE

➤ Have the LIFE YOU DESERVE

➤ Start YOUR JOURNEY

Go to www.profitablelandlordsystem.com and schedule your no obligation call to see if the Profitable Landlord System is your simple, repeatable and predictable system for getting the life you deserve! Now is the time to take that leap of faith and invest in yourself and your future!

CHAPTER 8:
THE PROFITABLE LANDLORD SYSTEM

We created the *Profitable Landlord System* to allow others the opportunity to become successful real estate investors. We are committed to the success of each person who commits to learning and following our map to financial freedom! Our journey is not perfect, and we continue to grow and learn with each deal. We will share our knowledge, tools, and experience with anyone interested in creating and building wealth to leave a legacy. Thank you for being part of this journey with us!

The courses in the Profitable Landlord System are based on real-life experiences and apply to anyone who has an interest in real estate investing, specifically single-family rentals. This is our bread and butter! Yes, we have flipped, wholesaled and owner financed properties. We also created and sold notes, but our financial freedom and independence came from investing in single-family rentals.

Individuals who desire financial freedom, early retirement, and enough time and resources to live the life of their dreams are perfect candidates for the Profitable Landlord System.

A profitable Landlord:

➢ Maintains a steady source of passive income.

➢ Reduces tax liability using the current tax laws that benefit real estate investors.

➢ Puts their money to work for them – builds on real estate investing, grows money through appreciation, monthly cash flow, and can leverage their portfolio for additional cash resources to purchase and invest in other real estate products.

➢ Controls their financial destiny through dedication and knowledge to continue growing their wealth.

➢ Successfully achieves their financial goals, secures ongoing wealth, leaves a legacy, and has an impact on their community.

My Top 3 Valuable Experiences

I want to share some of my experiences with you in hopes that these can help you avoid some of the riskier pitfalls of real estate investing.

1. People generally cannot figure out why they are stuck and need someone to tell them what to do or give them guidance to get unstuck. Real estate investors are highly driven, or want to be highly driven, but need a road map to get there or handholding to get the ball rolling.

2. No one will do it for you, and most people are too scared to even try. When we moved from Arizona to Texas, it was a scary time for us. We quit our jobs, sold our house, and uprooted our daughter. It was stressful and nerve-racking, but I believed that it was the right thing to do. I knew it would enhance our financial situation more in one year than we could by working for ten years. You have to believe in yourself when no one else will.

3. You have more credibility with people when you can show them you walk the talk. You must take calculated risks when you are growing your business, and basically fake it 'til you make it. Smiling through an uncomfortable situation is a

great way to overcome your fears. Concentrate on smiling, and you find yourself with a positive outward glow.

The Profitable Landlord System provides a step-by-step method to build wealth, which includes a thorough market analysis of a target property, potential rental income, and the ability to buy the property with terms that garner a steady rate of return. The PLS shows committed real estate entrepreneurs how they can create wealth and build a legacy for their family.

When we looked around for a program for real estate investors, we realized that no one in this industry has the exact step-by-step process written out in a straight-forward and easy manner. It takes more than buying a rental property to become wealthy. Building wealth requires a system to analyze the property, tenants, lenders, and managers to scale your landlord business: **The Profitable Landlord System.**

Our proprietary methodology is based on real-life experiences—good and bad—as our passion is to help landlords quickly and effortlessly have the tools to become profitable and avoid expensive financial missteps when investing in real estate.

The PLS includes case studies, examples, and core profitable indicators that landlords can apply to their existing portfolios or use them to add and assess their investments.

So, where should you start? First, review the problems that most people face when they start investing in real estate so that you can avoid these problems:

1. **Where to start** – Lack the knowledge to analyze and determine if a property will be profitable.

2. **Deal Flow** – Lack time or resources to adequately find profitable sellers. Don't first identify their profitable seller, the types of properties to focus on, where to look, and how to negotiate with a profitable seller.

3. **Tenant Screening and Management** – Unable to control repair costs because there is no system in place to deal with routine maintenance requests that are handled by a tenant (specifically, changing smoke detector batteries and air filters).

4. **Ongoing Funding** – Positioning themselves to find money to purchase properties because they lack financial knowledge and finesse to position themselves to attract profitable funders.

5. **Control** – Unwilling to hire a profitable property manager and work on scaling their business. Not setting KPIs to monitor team progress or lack tools to monitor teams' activities.

The Profitable Landlord System addresses each problem, covering:

- **Profitable Sellers**: Where are they and how do you find them

- **Profitable Tenants**: You can get the best property, without profitable tenants, it can cost you time and money

- **Profitable Funders**: Ways to pay for investment properties

- **Profitable Managers**: STEM Save time, energy, and money

- **Profitable Teams** – Achieve financial freedom and have time to enjoy your life

REAL ESTATE INVESTOR MINDSET

A real estate investor must have the proper mindset. You will experience many ups and downs in your journey. I will show you how I overcame many obstacles, but there were many times when I doubted my decisions.

Investing in real estate is not a cheap endeavor! Sure, there are ways to finance houses, but if someone tells you that you don't need any money, you should keep going. Real estate investing takes some money and time!

So, what mindset did I have to adopt? Here are some ways I focused on achieving my financial freedom:

❖ **New Mindset 1**: Consistent marketing is key. Good deals are out there, but you must identify the specific property type and strategy you want to incorporate so your message is focused.

❖ **New Mindset 2**: Become really good at one strategy like we did to become profitable landlords. We determined our formula for finding profitable sellers and stuck to that formula. Simple, repeatable, and predictable.

❖ **New Mindset 3**: Set a specific amount of time each day, week, month, etc., to find profitable sellers. A set amount of time each day to a dedicated marketing technique/strategy will result in a continual deal flow.

Visit my website www.ProfitableLandlordSystem.com to take the assessment and start your real estate investing journey today! The assessment will help you determine your ability and desire to be a profitable landlord. Do you have time and energy to start building the life you deserve?

To get all of the free downloads, simply follow the link to get them today to start you on your journey as a profitable landlord!

https://mailchi.mp/kbnhomes.com/qtnb5c13oe

About the Author

Nancy Wallace-Laabs is a licensed real estate broker in the state of Texas. She has more than 15 years of real estate investing experience, owns several rental properties, and was a property manager for more than 12 years in the North DFW area.

Nancy and her husband, Brian, founded the Profitable Landlord System to provide a predictable, repeatable, and simple step-by-step method for becoming a profitable landlord to help other real estate investors who want to create wealth, experience financial freedom, and leave an impact for their community. The Profitable Landlord System includes real-life examples, case studies, and risk factor considerations that every investor needs to be successful. Visit www.ProfitableLandlordSystem.com for your free assessment.

Nancy and Brian have pledged to donate 10% of all proceeds from the Profitable Landlord System to their non-profit Map of Hope. They founded this non-profit due to the effect mental health illness had on their lives – specifically, chronic depression.

You can read about Brian and Nancy's legacy at https://mapofhope.net.

If you or a loved one suffers from depression, and you want to make a difference, please consider making a donation to help someone that is suffering today. Your donation is tax deductible and will help someone get the treatment that will change their lives! Thank you! Your gift is appreciated.

DONATE NOW AT

www.MapOfHope.net